A Mississippi Whale Tale

The Story of Two Pygmy Killer Whales' Fight for Survival

M.H. Crawford, M. Samuelson, D. Moore

AuthorHouse™
1663 Liberty Drive
Bloomington, IN 47403
www.authorhouse.com
Phone: 1 (800) 839-8640

Published by AuthorHouse 05/17/2018

ISBN: 978-1-5462-1634-6 (sc)
ISBN: 978-1-5462-1635-3 (e)
ISBN: 978-1-5462-1636-0 (hc)

Library of Congress Control Number: 2017917271

Print information available on the last page.

This book is printed on acid-free paper.

"Some people, places, event sequences, or timeframe may have been modified for story purposes."

author**HOUSE**®

Acknowledgments

The Institute for Marine Mammal Studies (IMMS) staff and volunteers dedicated hundreds of hours around the clock to ensure the success of this rehabilitation. Dr. Moby Solangi provided resources and leadership throughout the rehabilitation process and acted as a liaison among the numerous agencies who assisted with this rehabilitation and release.

The stranding and veterinary team led by Drs. Connie Clemons Chevis, Debra Moore, and Eric Pulis, together with the animal care team led by Mr. Tim Hoffland and Mrs. Kelly Pulis, ensured that the animals received the appropriate diet, including fatty fish and squid, in addition to the necessary medications and fluids. The research team led by Drs. Jonathan Pitchford, Eric Pulis, and Mystera Samuelson collected behavioral and biological data relevant to the whales' rehabilitation in order to document this unique opportunity to study this rare species.

The rehabilitation and release of these two animals would not have been possible without a multi-agency collaboration. The US Navy Marine Mammal Program, US Coast Guard, Chicago Zoological Society, Cascadia Research Collective, National Marine Mammal Foundation, National Marine Fisheries Service/National Oceanic and Atmospheric Administration, Mississippi Department of Marine Resources, local law enforcement and fire departments, and the Mississippi State University College of Veterinary Medicine were essential to the treatment, rehabilitation, and eventual release of these animals.

In particular, Dr. Eric Jensen of the US Navy Marine Mammal Program and Dr. Jennifer Gambino of the Mississippi State University College of Veterinary Medicine were integral in forming the whales' treatment plan. Also Dr. Randy Wells of the Chicago Zoological Society's Sarasota Dolphin Research Program and Dr. Robin Baird of the Cascadia Research Collective provided much appreciated advice and assistance in evaluating the animals' behavior and planning for their release.

We would like to thank Dr. Nathan Hopper for his assistance with mapping the whales' movements post-release.

Of course, this effort would not have been possible without the help of countless volunteers who assisted in every step of the process.

We would also like to thank Kevin Lee for illustrating how the satellite tagging system works.

Chapter 1

Rescue

Shane wiped his fingers across his forehead, slinging the heavy sweat off the side of the boat. He shaded his eyes as he gazed toward the sun. He knew it would be another hot Southern Mississippi day. He maneuvered his boat through the marsh and listened to the sounds of great blue herons while the morning sun stretched over the Bay of Saint Louis.

Shane settled into one of his favorite fishing spots, baited his hook, and tossed it off the side of the boat into the water. It landed with a small splash below the reeds. He smiled at his perfectly placed toss and said, "There's gotta be a fish there."

The air was muggy, and the gnats were biting their way through his clothes, but the Mississippi coast was his favorite place. It was home. Shane knew his boat and the bay with all its special fishing holes well. He drew in a deep breath of fresh air, savored the brackish taste for a moment, and released it when he heard an unusual, loud sound.

Puhh … Shhha!

"What?" Shane whispered, swinging his head from side to side, trying to identify its source.

Puhh … Shhha!

Shane heard it again. Anxiously, he reeled in his line. Then he moved the boat around a bend toward the noise.

Puhh … Shhha!

The sound reminded Shane of a scuba diver taking a deep breath. As he moved closer, the sound grew louder. He leaned forward, squinting against the bright sun, but the needlerush grass concealed the sound's source.

As he turned around the next grassy bend, his eyes widened at a twitchy, jerking motion in the black mud ahead. Leaning forward, he noticed a black body directly in front of him. As it lifted its head, Shane saw frantic eyes staring up at him.

"What's that!?" Shane gasped.

Unable to move, the whales were trapped in thick marsh.

The animal jerked again, throwing muddy sludge with its flat tail. Shane realized he was looking at some kind of dolphin stranded on the mudflat. It needed help … and fast.

"Where's that card?" He searched his backpack, throwing hooks onto the boat's floor. Shane plunged deeper into the bag until he finally found his wallet.

Puhh … Shhha!

He heard it again as his boat drifted toward the marshy bank. His hand shook as he flipped open his wallet, found the card, and read: 1-888-SOS-DOLPHIN. As fast as he could, he dialed the number that would connect him to the local marine stranded-mammal hotline.

The phone rang for what seemed like an eternity until a voice came through. "The Institute for Marine Mammals stranding hotline. This is Alicia. Can I help you?"

"Uh, I'm in Bay St. Louis, and I found a … black dolphin!" Shane said.

"You found a what?" Alicia asked.

"Uh, yes, ma'am. A black dolphin," Shane replied.

"Okay," Alicia said. "I'm going to need more information from you, like the animal's description, its injuries, and your GPS coordinates. Then I can send someone out there to help."

Puhh … Shhha!

The sound made Shane spin around and scan the muddy water. He paused for a moment and held his breath.

"Sir?" Alicia asked.

"Yeah, yeah. I'm here," Shane said.

Puhh … Shhhaa!

A small spray dispersed above the black mound. Shane's mouth dropped open in amazement as he noticed another black lump completely on land near a patch of reeds.

"There's another one!" he nearly yelled into the phone.

"Did you say you see a second dolphin?" Alicia asked.

"I think so, but this one's out of the water," Shane replied.

"Okay." Alicia looked at her phone and reached for her pen. "Give me your exact coordinates so I can get help." She took down the numbers as fast as Shane read them off of the boat's GPS navigator. "Okay. We're on our way!"

"Please hurry." Shane turned back to the black dolphin at his feet, parted the reeds, and revealed its extensive wounds. "They may not live very long."

The whales had become completely trapped on land.

For the first time since Shane found the dolphins, hope rose in his chest as two rescue boats came through the marsh, followed by two Jet Skis.

"Help is here." Shane smiled at the animals and then looked back up at the IMMS rescue team. "*Over here!*" he yelled.

The boat captain saw him immediately and steered toward Shane. Within moments, the team jumped out into the muddy water. The splashes caused the first animal to thrash from side to side as it sought to find freedom in deeper water. The rescuers rushed to the animal.

Shane noticed some confusion in their eyes. "Is it bad? Does it look worse than you thought?" He looked back over the animal's injuries.

The lead veterinarian, Dr. Connie Chevis, spoke up, "This isn't a bottlenose dolphin."

"I don't understand," Shane said.

Scattered voices drifted through the rescuers as individuals attempted to identify the animal.

"It's a whale, I think," the veterinarian replied. "Maybe a melon-headed whale or pygmy killer whale. It's surely not a bottlenose dolphin, but both whale species are types of toothed dolphins. The most obvious clue is the animal's color. It's much darker than a bottlenose dolphin. Also this animal lacks a long, pointy rostrum. This whale has a broad, rounded rostrum."

Puhh … Shhha!

Once again, the small whale floundered in the shallow water, causing mud to cake farther over it wounds.

"The wounds are really bad." Dr. Chevis looked at the animal care director. "Its chances of surviving the trip back to IMMS are slim. Even if they make it, we'll have to treat their wounds and possible infections. Not to mention the fact that scientists know very little about these animals." She shook her head and looked at the marsh around them. "And why are they here in the first place? These animals are found in deep waters. I just don't know if they can survive."

As she expressed her concerns, the whale thrashed, showing them that it was not ready to give up just yet.

Without another word, the veterinarian said, "We need a stretcher immediately. We have to try." Determination grew in her eyes. "They deserve for us to give them a fighting chance. Hand me that bag. We'll need to administer some emergency medications."

"I'm on it," another rescuer spoke up.

Shane recognized her voice at once. *Alicia*, he thought.

Alicia climbed into the boat and proceeded to hand out stretchers and other veterinary supplies.

"Where's the other whale?" Tim, another rescuer, asked as he waded through the water.

His knee-high boots failed him as the water and mud flowed over the brim, saturating his feet. Shane watched as the rescue team acted in unison. He knew these stranded animals' survival relied on each person to act quickly on their behalf.

The IMMS team struggled through the marsh mud in order to get the whale back onto the boat.

"Over there!" Shane pointed in the animal's direction.

Puhhh … Shhha!

The other whale breathed as if on cue, and Tim watched the water droplets clear from its blowhole.

Although Tim tried to hurry to the second whale's side, the mud bogged him down with each step. When he finally reached the animal, he realized the severity of the situation. The whale had managed to sink almost completely into the quicksand-like mud with only its blowhole exposed.

"Heart rate is weak but stable," Dr. Chevis said at the side of the first whale. "However, its respirations are labored! We need to get it on our boat for better monitoring."

"I'm gonna need help over here!" Tim yelled.

He clawed at the mud surrounding the whale. Each handful revealed more and more of the whale until he could finally reach underneath it.

The team knew their task was not going to be easy. Each whale weighed approximately three hundred pounds, and they were sitting in deep mud. They placed each animal in a stretcher. Every time the team moved the whale a foot, their boots sank a foot into the mud. They pulled away from the suction over and over. For an hour, the rescuers hauled the animal a foot at a time, struggling to yank their boots from the mud.

Finally their hard work paid off. Both whales were lying on a mat in the IMMS boat with a care team designated for each. The teams continued checking their vital signs and reflexes.

"Heart rate seventy-two beats per minute!" Dr. Debra Moore, another veterinarian with IMMS, yelled. More readings followed. "Breaths are averaging three to four per minute!"

"We have to get moving if we want to give them a chance at all!" another team member said. "Let's get going!"

Wet towels were placed on the animals to keep them cool.

The whales sat on the foam mat, protected from the sun by wet cloth, as veterinarians assessed their condition.

The boat growled to a start and rushed back to the marina. A group of more IMMS team members stood at the dock, waiting to lend fresh hands. Each whale required six people to lift it from the boat. The next objective was to get the animals to the rescue van and transport them back to the IMMS facility.

Staff, interns, and volunteers helped to move the whales from the boats to the trucks, so they could be transported back to IMMS.

Monitoring the whales' vitals paused briefly while each was lifted into the van. Once they were situated, every minute, every response, and every moment was recorded.

Someone said, "I'm not sure these are melon-headed whales. They seem different, but definitely not like anything we have studied or seen around here before."

The statement went unnoticed as the team checked and rechecked the whales' conditions. For now, their only focus was to keep the whales alive. After what seemed like an eternity, the team reached the Institute for Marine Mammal Studies in Gulfport, Mississippi, to find that more volunteers and staff were waiting to help.

"One, two, three." The team lifted both whales from the truck next to an above-ground pool that had been prepared for the whales.

IMMS staff, interns, and volunteers helped to lift the whales from the truck to the rehabilitation pool for treatment.

Each whale was once again given a team and lowered onto a foam mat near the hospital. Veterinarians, staff, and volunteers proceeded to take blood, fecal, stomach, and urine samples from each whale. This information allowed the veterinarians to assess the whales' health, so they could decide how to best treat the animals. The whales were clearly members of a very rarely observed species, which meant the veterinarians knew little about them. The staff was in uncharted territory and would need all of the information they could get.

Although weak, each whale fought for freedom, thrashing throughout the exams.

"Okay! We have everything we need," Dr. Chevis said. "Let's get them back in water ASAP!" She pointed to all the volunteers and repeated, "Let's get them into the water! We need to keep them calm."

Tim said, "Okay, we need six people in the water to receive the whales and another six people to lift the animal over the edge of the pool. A second group can stay on the other animal until we are ready."

Immediately the team lifted the whales back onto the stretchers and carried them over to the quarantine pool as more volunteers hopped into the water to receive them. The whales were too weak to move on their own.

"Keep them at the surface so they can breathe. I would like volunteers to take shifts walking them around in the pool," Dr. Chevis spoke again. "It may be impossible for them to float or swim to the surface to breathe. They are also likely disoriented. Since their muscles are weak and injured, they will need us to support them. They are dehydrated, their skin is badly damaged, and they could get stressed out in this new environment. The next twenty-four to forty-eight hours are the most critical. If they live until tomorrow, they might just have a chance."

One hour passed as the volunteers continued to hold the whales at the surface. As they worked, they were careful to make sure the whales could see one another. This visual contact seemed to help the animals remain calm. Both animals continued to breathe.

The hours rolled by throughout the night while staff and volunteers took shifts holding up the whales for air. Some noticed the whales continuously watching one another and occasionally making whistling sounds. Although initially the whales were assigned numbers to help identify them, they were later given the names Marco and Polo, after the children's game, as they constantly kept tabs on where the other one was.

The whales were supported around the clock to ensure they could breathe. The team wore masks to protect themselves from potential diseases the whales could carry.

Chapter 2

The Rehabilitation

"Did they survive the night?" Victoria, another rescuer, asked anxiously preparing to hear the worst.

"Yes, they did, and they are able to swim a little on their own!" Tim said enthusiastically. "We are going to try feeding them again."

Over the night, rescuers had offered fish to the whales, but neither animal opened his mouth to eat. Either from fear, shock, or some unknown reason, their mouths remained clamped shut.

IMMS staff helped to ensure the whales were able to breathe by holding them up in the water.

"It's clear that we have to try a different approach. They're too weak and too nervous to eat," Dr. Moby Solangi said. "We'll have to hand-feed the whales today, or we might lose them."

Five team members joined the volunteer holding Polo and carried him over to Tim at the pool's edge. Fortunately, local firefighters had come to assist IMMS staff in supporting the whales.

"Make sure you hold on tight." Tim had wrapped his hands in towels and tape to protect him from the whale's teeth. "Polo's not gonna like this, but we have to help him eat if he's going to survive."

Dr. Moore nodded in agreement. "Yes," she spoke as she directed volunteers to help. "The whales' throats are different from ours in a couple of key ways. They breathe a little differently than we do, and they do not have a gag reflex. It won't hurt them, but they won't like being handled."

The six firefighters nodded and wrapped their arms tightly around Polo. Although injured, the whales were still very powerful animals. The rescue team would need extra strength to hold the whales in place as they received care. The firefighters became the perfect complement to the IMMS medical staff.

Tim pried open Polo's mouth, hesitating as the whale's pearly white teeth waited for him to put in his hand. With his free hand, Tim placed a herring into the whale's throat. Polo squirmed, causing the men to tighten their grip for a moment as he swallowed the fish.

Tim chuckled. "That's one down, but he still needs a lot more to eat if he wants to survive." He glanced down at a stainless steel bucket filled with more fish, knowing they were in for a long feeding session. Once both Marco and Polo had eaten, the team let them rest before focusing on hydration.

The team used a tube to deliver much needed hydration to Polo with the help of the local fire department and veterinary technician.

Like most marine mammals, Marco and Polo got their water from the fish they ate. They could not drink the ocean water, as it was too salty and could prove fatal if too much were ingested. During their rehabilitation, the whales would need supplemental water because their food had been frozen, which caused it to have less water than live fish. This left two options. The whales needed to either eat water-filled gelatin balls, a lot like Jell-O snacks but without sugar or flavoring. Or they would need to drink fresh water through a tube with the help of the rehabilitators.

For now, the rescuers needed to use a tube to hydrate the whales because they were too weak to eat the gelatin on their own. Just like with feeding, the whales' special throats ensured that passing the hydration tube was not painful. However, it would help to save their lives.

Several days passed, and IMMS team members stood around the pool, ready for the morning feeding.

Before the veterinarians announced the day's plans, Dr. Solangi stepped up and spoke, "We have confirmed that the whales are pygmy killer whales, not melon-headed whales, although they are very similar species."

The words brought a smile to his face. "This species has rarely—if ever—been successfully rehabilitated. They seemed to have strayed hundreds of miles off course where they normally live. We are learning valuable information about their biology and behavior. And if they can be released, we may have the opportunity to learn much more about these animals and their lives in the Gulf of Mexico."

Dr. Solangi pulled out a folded email from his pocket. "I have even more interesting information here." He unfolded the paper and read it aloud, "Regarding the genetics of your *Feresa* samples, there is a high probability that these two whales are related."

The paper crackled as Dr. Solangi folded it back up. "There is more data on their relationship, but ultimately they could be half-brothers. This makes sense to me. Marco acts like an older brother protecting Polo. Without each other, they could not hope to survive."

Dr. Solangi continued, "Dolphin and whale strandings are a big curiosity to people. We know that sometimes they are extremely sick, but at other times healthy animals will follow their sick leaders to strand on land. Even when we push them back, they will still come right back onto shore and die. These two have probably been together for a large part of their lives and are likely very close, which would help explain their genetic similarities and why they stranded together."

Tim responded, "Well, that explains why Marco and Polo always want to swim together, touch each other, and often rest side by side throughout the day and night."

The heat of the summer turned into a cool South Mississippi autumn. During that time, Marco and Polo's hydration improved, but their skin infections grew more severe. Antibiotics alone were not working, so the veterinary staff found other ways to complement their current treatments.

"Let's examine the wounds on his side." Dr. Chevis discussed with Dr. Moore. She drew in a deep breath and pointed out the whales' wounds. "He was in the sun for much too long, and his skin dried. This resulted in a severe sunburn." She assessed Polo's skin. "Honey has great healing qualities, but first we are going to cleanse these wounds, and he is not going to like it. We will then use laser therapy to speed up the healing process, and finally we'll put the honey on them."

Drs. Chevis and Moore used a laser to treat the whales' wounds while others
helped them stay above the surface of the water, in order to breathe.

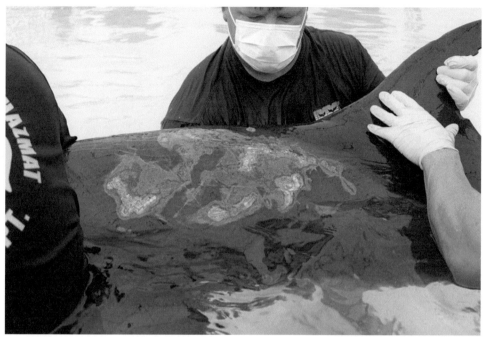

The whales' wounds slowly began to heal with treatment, but this was a long process.

Veterinarians continued administering therapeutic treatments such as laser therapy to help these extensive wounds to heal.

The team watched as the whales grew stronger every day.

As time and care healed their wounds, the whales' strength grew. Spring was just around the corner. Both Marco and Polo felt better, and their need for medication lessened. They also began eating on their own. Both whales took fish from staff without the need of support from the volunteers in the water. The hope for their release back into the wild became a very real possibility, yet the whales still were not ready.

To be released, the whales needed to be evaluated to ensure they could survive in the wild. This had not been done before, so IMMS caretakers, scientists, and veterinarians worked hard to assess both their health and behavior. They also consulted with governmental officials and other world-renowned experts throughout this process.

If released back into the Gulf of Mexico, Marco and Polo needed to be able to hunt, communicate, and find their home. Pygmy killer whales, like so many other dolphin species, required excellent hearing to do both.

A caregiver watched proudly as Polo accepted a fish, and ate it on his own.

21

Dr. Houser (hearing specialist) of National Marine Mammal Foundation tested
Polo's hearing with the assistance of IMMS veterinarians and caregivers.

"Today we will find out if our whales can hear," Dr. Dorian Houser said. "By placing electrodes behind the blowhole, we can measure their ear's and brain's response to sound. Hearing is extremely valuable for them. They need it to communicate with other whales and to echolocate on objects and prey. Without good hearing, it would be difficult for them to survive back in the open ocean."

The team remained silent over the next hour while Dr. Houser glanced back and forth between the computer screen and the whales.

"I have good news," Dr. Houser finally said, putting away his equipment. "Each whale has sufficient hearing for release."

The team celebrated as they now knew that the whales were one step closer to being released back into the Gulf of Mexico and one step closer to freedom. But the question still remained if they were strong enough to swim and survive out in the Gulf of Mexico.

The days of healing rolled by, and summer came. The whales fought through their illnesses and ailments, gaining strength with each passing day. Some days were worse than others. The veterinarians and staff had to make sure that they responded quickly, diagnosing and treating both whales when they showed any signs of illness. Through it all, the brothers helped one another. If Polo became too weak to dive down, Marco stayed by his side. If Marco became sick, Polo stayed at his side.

"Today is a great day!" Dr. Solangi, president of IMMS, smiled at the team assembled around him. "The whales have been eating well, and their infections have nearly cleared up. We're getting closer each day to releasing them back into the Gulf of Mexico. To allow them more room to move and heal, we'll be moving them to a deeper pool today. I need everyone to stay safe today as we move Marco and Polo. Each whale will have an attending team. We'll place them on stretchers, load them into a truck, and move them to their new home."

Rehabilitators celebrated the whales' successful move into the bigger pool.

It wasn't long before Marco and Polo began diving down ten feet to the pool floor. Their muscles grew stronger with every movement.

Throughout the rehabilitation process, the IMMS research team, led by Drs. Pitchford and Samuelson, collected behavioral data by recording each movement and sound the whales made. This data would help the scientists learn more about this rare species.

As Marco and Polo grew stronger, they began to play. They chased each other around and occasionally jumped high into the air before landing with a huge splash on their sides, sending water flying in all directions. Scientists had called this behavior "breaching," and it had been seen by dolphins and whales in the ocean.

As the whales' health improved, they became more active and were often seen breaching and playing together under the early Summer sun.

As the whales became healthier, their bond became more evident.

Chapter 3

The Release, July 11, 2016

After ten months of good days and bad days, it was time to release Marco and Polo out into the Gulf of Mexico. IMMS staff, firefighters, US Coast Guard, and US Navy Marine Mammal Program personnel, who had worked tirelessly for months, assembled one final time to accomplish their ultimate task.

"I can't tell you how excited I am to see this day." Dr. Solangi said as a smile crossed his face. "None of this would be possible without everyone's help. So many people gave of their time and their hearts. You have all been vital to Marco and Polo's survival." His eyes scanned the crowd, connecting with as many people as possible. "They have come so far together. We have seen them play, swim, and support one another. These two animals are stronger together than if they had been apart. Likewise, our teamwork kept them alive. This is a victory for all of us!"

Some of the crowd nodded while one firefighter patted another volunteer on the back.

Dr. Solangi continued, "But it's not time to celebrate just yet. We have to transport them to the ship and then to the release site. As always, stay focused today." His voice turned from triumph to concerned, and he furrowed his eyebrows together. "Marco and Polo have overcome so much, but they can still be overwhelmed by the stress on their eight-hour-long journey to their home out in the deep Gulf of Mexico. Stress can quickly threaten their survival, and they could die. Our goal is to keep them as calm as possible. If we do this, we might just have a successful release."

The team nodded as they turned to focus on Marco and Polo.

"Okay then. Let's get to work. You all know your assignments. Let's go!" Dr. Solangi said.

A hush fell over the team as they worked to move each whale. Marco and Polo once again had a team designated to them, just like when they arrived. Six people carried, two people collected vital signs, and each whale had his own designated veterinarian.

The team helped to hold Polo up, as veterinarians gave him one last exam before transport.

Keeping track of heartbeats and respiration was important to assessing the whales' health during transport. Here, Drs. Moore (IMMS) and Jensen (U.S. Navy Marine Mammal Program) prepared to assess Polo's health with an EKG. Still, no time was lost as the team assess heart rate manually, by placing a hand under the animal's side pectoral fin, while the equipment was set up.

The trip to the harbor was short compared to their arrival. The massive Coast Guard ship, *The Cypress*, awaited them, and a crane lifted both three-hundred-pound whales onto the ship. Marco had gained twenty five pounds, and Polo gained forty four pounds during their rehabilitation. Excitement rippled through the vessel because history was being made and the forty-two crewmembers who were excited to assist.

The U.S. Coast Guard cutter, The Cypress, docked in Gulfport Harbor.

Personnel from the U.S. Navy Marine Mammal Program assisted IMMS staff in every aspect of the transport, including loading them onto The Cypress.

After the crew loaded the whales onto the ship, the buoy deck provided the team space to monitor each whale. Technicians connected EKG electrodes to Marco and Polo to monitor their heart rates and to listen to their breaths. Meanwhile staff scooped water from each whale's carrier to keep their skin moist.

To ensure the animals were released as close to their natural habitat as possible, the whales needed to be released in at least a thousand feet of water, which was a hundred miles from Gulfport. As deep-water animals, Marco and Polo likely felt most at home just past the continental shelf where they could swim and hunt in the depths.

Eight hours passed as the ship travelled over the Gulf of Mexico's beautiful waters, reaching the target depth at 5:03 p.m. The critical moment finally came, and the whales were prepped for their release. The team hoisted the whales out of their containers and onto foam mats, located on the ship's deck.

The team monitored the whales' health closely because a spike in stress now could still mean trouble. For months, Marco and Polo had helped one another lessen the curse of stress, so the team made sure to lay them within sight of each other. Health checks were made, and veterinarians gave the final approval for the whales' release.

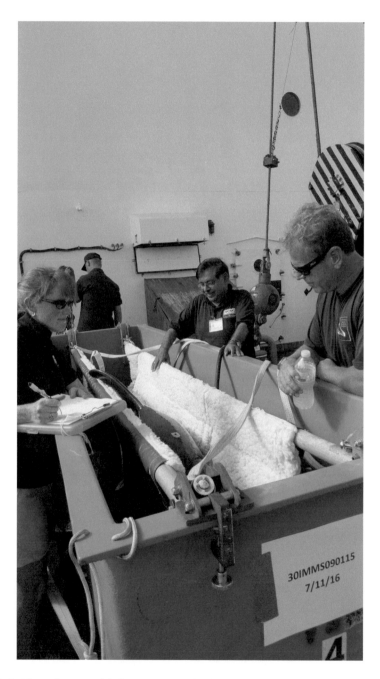

30IMMS090115
7/11/16

4

The whales' breathing and behavior were closely monitored throughout their journey.

The veterinary team examined the EKG to assess Marco's health throughout the transport.

The whales were fitted with satellite tags that the veterinarians had attached to their dorsal fins. IMMS and other scientists hoped the tags would help them assess the whales' habits and movement long after their release.

*IMMS and U.S. Navy Marine Mammal Program personnel prepared
the whales for release back into the Gulf of Mexico.*

The world knew very little about pygmy killer whales before Marco and Polo stranded in Bay St. Louis, and the IMMS team recorded massive amounts of information throughout their recovery.

"Okay. It's time to put these guys back into their home." Dr. Eric Jensen, head veterinarian from the US Navy Marine Mammal Program, said. He directed the teams to cradle each whale in his specialized foam mat and to lift him to the ship's ledge. He smiled and drew in a deep breath. "I am going to count from three to one. When I get to one, I want those on the back of the mat to lift and gently slide Marco into the water." He lifted his hand and counted, "Three … two … one!"

The team lifted, and Marco slid back into the water. They held their breath for a moment because he didn't move. The team watched as his eyes scanned the open water around him. Once he realized he was home, his fluke kicked forcefully, propelling him into the depths.

U.S. Navy Marine Mammal Program and Coast Guard personnel helped to lift
the whales into the water as IMMS and NOAA staff cheered.

The team waited a moment to be sure Marco was out of the way before helping Polo. Crewmembers watched as Marco resurfaced and waited for his brother to slide off the mat and dive back into the water.

Once the animals were together, Marco took one last look up at *The Cypress*. The team cheered, patted each other on the back, and released a collective sigh of relief to see the healthy whales back home.

Marco took one last look at The Cypress, and the people who helped bring him home.

Polo turned to restart his life in the wild. He brought with him a satellite tag, which will help scientists to understand his life in the northern Gulf of Mexico.

Polo had come so far in last the ten months. He had nearly died numerous times, but many humans gave their time, support, and hearts so he could survive. He, too, gave the ship one last long gaze before the rare creature ventured off with his brother. They would live the rest of their lives at home in the Gulf of Mexico.

When *The Cypress* returned to port around midnight, Dr. Eric Pulis received the first notification that the whales' tags had communicated with the satellite. Marco and Polo had left the release site and were travelling together.

Back on land, the staff and volunteers who had assisted in the rescue and rehabilitation were thrilled to hear that the whales had been successfully released back to their home in the Gulf of Mexico. Dr. Pulis, supervisor of the IMMS stranding program, and his team would continue monitoring the whales' satellite tag transmissions to see where they would go in their travels. They soon observed that the whales traveled approximately two hundred miles to the Mississippi Canyon and were diving over a thousand feet into the water to hunt for the food they had been accustomed to eating all of their lives.

This was a proud moment for not only the IMMS staff, but the hard work that all cetacean rehabilitation centers do around the world. It was also a very proud moment for all Mississippians as well. Without the help of so many in our State, the success of Marco and Polo's rescue, rehabilitation and release would not have been possible.

Basic Map to MS Canyon

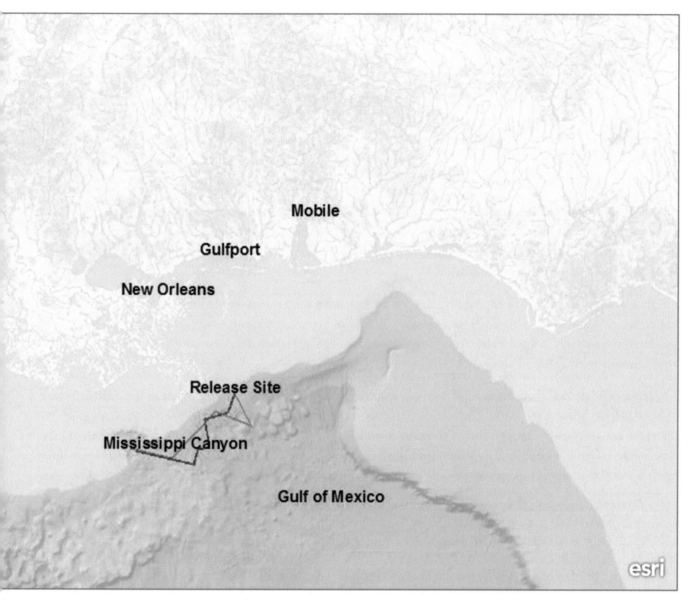

Mobile

Gulfport

New Orleans

Release Site

Mississippi Canyon

Gulf of Mexico

esri

For three days after being released, Marco (demonstrated by the green line) and Polo (demonstrated by the red line) swam throughout the Mississippi Canyon.

Chapter 4

More Information about Pygmy Killer Whales

Cetaceans are marine mammals that include whales, dolphins, and porpoises. They are divided into two groups: Odontoceti have teeth used to catch prey such as fish or other mammals; and Mysticeti have baleen used to filter krill and other small prey from the water.

Pygmy killer whales (*Feresa attenuata*) are toothed whales and members of the dolphin family. They are related to the better-known killer whale, or orca, but are more closely related to melon-headed whales, pilot whales, and false killer whales. All of these species are members of the same family, and you can see the resemblance in their long, sleek body shape and dark coloration.

Originally scientists at IMMS thought the pygmy killer whales were melon-headed whales, as both are around the same size. However, pygmy killer whales have telltale white markings around their mouths, which ultimately indicated the animals' true identity upon closer investigation. Genetic testing later confirmed that the animals were indeed pygmy killer whales.

Scientists estimate that there are around between approximately 150 to 400 of these whales in the northern Gulf of Mexico.[1,2,3] Although pygmy killer whales are present in tropical/subtropical open water environments globally, sightings are very rare.[4] Through limited observations, it is evident that this is a social species, living in groups that average around nine animals, although group size can range from two individuals to over thirty. There have been few observations of this species feeding in the wild, thus very little is known about their natural diet. This

[1] Barlow, (2006). Cetacean abundance in Hawaiian waters estimated from a summer/fall survey in 2002. Marine Mammal Science, 22(2), 446-464.

[2] Mullin, K. D., & Fulling, G. L. (2004). Abundance of cetaceans in the oceanic northern Gulf of Mexico 1996-2001. Marine Mammal Science, 20(4), 787-807.

[3] Taylor, B. L., Baird, R., Barlow, J., Dawson, S. M., Ford, J., Mead, J. G., Notarbartolo di Sciara, G., Wade, P., & Pitman, R. L. (2008). Feresa attenuata. The IUCN Red List of Threatened Species. eT8551A12921135. http://dx.doi.org/10.2305/IUCN.UK.2008.RLTS.T8551A12921135.en.

[4] Waring, G. T., Josephson, E., Maze-Foley, K., & Rosel, P. E. (2013). U.S. Atlantic and Gulf of Mexico Marine Mammal Stock Assessments – 2012. NOAA Tech Memo NMFS NE 223; 419 p.

5. Baird, R. (2016). Pygmy killer whales (Feresa attenuata). The Lives of Hawai'i's Dolphins and Whales: Natural History and Conservation. University of Hawai'i Press: Honolulu, HI

could be due to a tendency to feed at night.[5] The little that is known of pygmy killer whale physiology has been learned through the examination of deceased individuals who have been stranded.[5] Thus, IMMS veterinarians, scientists, animal care staff, and consultants had very little data to inform the rescue efforts described in this book.

Through IMMS leadership, veterinary and animal care interventions, and support from both private and public sectors, the entire IMMS team was able to do what very few have done before, to successfully rehabilitate and release two pygmy killer whales.

Throughout the rehabilitation process, IMMS learned significant information about the animals' behavior and physiology, which was meticulously documented to inform future rehabilitation efforts and enhance our scientific understanding of this species. Critical factors such as species communication, social interactions, and activity levels were studied. Lifesaving medical aspects included maintaining a healthy hydration and nutritional status, diagnosing and treating day-to-day health crisis quickly and efficiently, and understanding the importance of the close social bond between Marco and Polo were vital.

As in humans and many other animals in the animal kingdom, the interactions among all of the above are critically important to our own survival, and these whales serve to remind us of how important it is for other species as well. With this knowledge, researchers may be able to intervene and save more stranded animals in the future as well as better inform future conservation efforts for wild pygmy killer whales in the northern Gulf of Mexico.

Upon release, the IMMS team was able to continue learning from the animals' movements through the use of satellite tags. These tags were applied to the dorsal fins of the animals prior to release and transmitted position, as well as dive depth and duration. This information not only provides insight into where these animals travel in the northern Gulf of Mexico, but also how and where they dive for their food. It was most interesting to see these two whales travel nearly two hundred miles from the release site to the Mississippi Canyon. This could mean that the animals were familiar with the area and somehow knew exactly where to go.

The whales' satellite tags communicated with a satellite which then transmitted to a scientist on shore.

Chapter 5

Strandings

The stranding (or beaching) of cetaceans is a phenomenon that has occurred throughout and likely beyond human history. It occurs when a cetacean physically strands itself on land and cannot return to its normal aquatic habitat. When a stranding occurs, as in the case of Marco and Polo, they will usually die without human intervention. These animals are extremely heavy, and without the buoyancy of the water, their weight makes it difficult for them to breathe and carry out other physiological functions outside of the water. Cetaceans are equipped with a thick blubber, or fat layer, which protects and insulates them from the cold water they live in. However, outside of the water, their blubber layer begins to immediately work against them, causing them to quickly overheat in the hot sun. Without eating, stranded whales and dolphins also become dehydrated very quickly, as wild cetaceans receive their water through the food they consume. In addition, their blowholes can become embedded in the sand or mud, making it impossible to breathe, causing them to suffocate.

Dolphins and many whales have very close-knit social bonds, and as with Marco and Polo, they can be seen interacting together, touching, and swimming in pairs. Many theories exist, which attempt to explain why they strand, but the phenomenon is still not completely understood.

Strandings can be related to illness, injury, or considerable old age. A sick or diseased animal can be vulnerable or debilitated, which prevents it from properly navigating the oceans. Environmental contaminants or toxic substances not only cause significant illness but also can lead to stranding events. Other reasons are associated with animals following the group members and changes to the environment that interrupt their navigation.

The Institute for Marine Mammal Studies protects and recues many different marine animals within the Gulf of Mexico. Learn more at www.imms.org.

About the Author

Each author has a unique skill set to help protect the marine life in the Gulf of Mexico. M. H. Crawford is an animal care and rescue and rehabilitation specialist at the Institute for Marine Mammal Studies. Dr. Mystera M. Samuelson is the lead research scientist, and Dr. Debra P. Moore, DVM, is one of the amazing veterinarians on staff at the institute.

About the Book

Two pygmy killer whales find themselves on a South Mississippi marsh bank, hundreds of miles from their deep-water home. A blistering sun, twisting streams, and towering grass surround them. Their survival seems bleak at best until a fishermen happens to see them stranded and unable to swim. He calls the Institute for Marine Mammals Studies Stranding hotline, and their odds for survival turn from dark to hopeful.

Printed in the United States
By Bookmasters